RIDDLES

Compiled by Pam Rosenberg

Illustrated by Mernie Gallagher-Cole

The Child's World

Published by The Child's World®
1980 Lookout Drive
Mankato, MN 56003-1705
800-599-READ
www.childsworld.com

The Child's World®: Mary Berendes, Publishing Director
Editorial Directions, Inc.: E. Russell Primm, Editorial
Director; Lucia Raatma, Copyeditor and Proofreader;
Jennifer Zeiger and Joshua Gregory, Editorial Assistants
The Design Lab: Design and production

Library of Congress Cataloging-in-Publication Data
Riddles / compiled by Pam Rosenberg ;
illustrated by Mernie Gallagher-Cole.
     p. cm.
  ISBN 978-1-60253-523-7 (library bound : alk. paper)
  1. Riddles, Juvenile. I. Rosenberg, Pam. II. Gallagher-
Cole, Mernie. III. Title.
  PN6371.5.R536 2010
  818'.60208—dc22   2010002053

Printed in the United States of America
Mankato, Minnesota
July 2010
F11538

ABOUT THE AUTHOR
Pam Rosenberg is the author of more than 50 books for children. She lives near Chicago, Illinois, with her husband and two children.

ABOUT THE ILLUSTRATOR
Mernie Gallagher-Cole lives in Pennsylvania with her husband and two children. She has illustrated many books for The Child's World®.

TABLE OF CONTENTS

WHAT?

Q: What begins with an E and ends with an E but only has one letter in it?
A: An envelope.

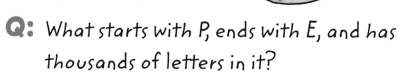

Q: What starts with P, ends with E, and has thousands of letters in it?
A: The post office.

Q: What do sea monsters eat?
A: Fish and ships.

Q: What's smarter than a talking parrot?
A: A spelling bee.

Q: What do snakes do after they have an argument?
A: They hiss and make up.

Q: What monster likes to dance?
A: The boogie man.

Q: What's a cheetah's favorite food?
A: Fast food.

Q: What's a mummy's favorite kind of music?
A: Wrap music.

Q: What's gray and has big ears and a trunk?
A: A mouse going on vacation.

Q: What do frogs like to eat with their hamburgers?
A: French flies.

Q: What kinds of stones are never found in the ocean?
A: Dry ones.

Q: What city has no people?
A: Electricity.

Q: What's always at the end of a rainbow?
A: The letter W.

Q: What do you find at the center of Paris?
A: The letter R.

Q: What has 88 keys but not a single door?
A: A piano.

Q: What kind of building always has the most stories?
A: A library.

Q: What occurs once in a minute, twice in a moment, and never in a thousand years?
A: The letter M.

Q: What has wheels and flies?
A: A garbage truck.

Q: What goes up but never comes down?
A: Your age.

Q: What is black and white, black and white, black and white?

A: A penguin rolling down a hill.

Q: What can clap but has no hands?

A: Thunder.

Q: Which is faster, heat or cold?

A: Heat—you can catch a cold.

Q: What has a ring but no finger?

A: A telephone.

Q: What comes up when the rain goes down?

A: An umbrella.

Q: What is put on the table and cut, but never eaten?

A: A deck of cards.

Q: What is full of holes but still holds water?

A: A sponge.

Q: What did one elevator say to the other?
A: I think I'm coming down with something.

Q: What did the sea say to the shore?
A: Nothing, it just waved.

Q: What did the envelope say to the stamp?
A: Stick with me and we'll go places.

Q: What's easy to get into and hard to get out of?
A: Trouble.

Q: What can fly but has no wings?
A: Time.

Q: What travels all around the world but stays in one corner?
A: A postage stamp.

Q: What gets wetter as it dries?
A: A towel.

Q: What has four eyes but cannot see?
A: The Mississippi.

....

Q: What can you catch but never throw?
A: A cold.

....

Q: What's brown and sticky?
A: A stick.

Q: What did one math book say to the other math book?
A: Have I got problems!

Q: What holds the moon up?
A: Moon-beams.

Q: What is the laziest mountain in the world?
A: Mount Ever-rest.

Q: What should you do if your puppy chews on your dictionary?
A: Take the words right out of his mouth.

Q: What sits at the bottom of the ocean and shakes?
A: A nervous wreck.

Q: What's a three-letter word for a mousetrap?
A: Cat.

Q: What has eight wheels and carries only one passenger?
A: A pair of roller skates.

WHAT DO YOU GET?

Q: What do you get when you cross a snowman with a wolf?
A: Frostbite.

Q: What do you get when 20 rabbits step backward?
A: A receding hare line.

Q: What do you get when you cross a piranha with a flower?
A: I don't know, but I wouldn't try to smell it if I were you!

11

Q: What do you get when you cross a centipede with a chicken?

A: Enough drumsticks for an army.

. . . .

Q: What do you get when a young goat falls into a blender?

A: A mixed-up kid.

Q: What do you get when you put corn holders into sweet corn?

A: Pierced ears.

Q: What do you get when you cross a sheep with a porcupine?

A: An animal that knits its own sweaters.

....

Q: What do you get if you cross a pirate with Santa Claus?

A: Yo-ho-ho-ho!

....

Q: What do you get when you walk through a field of four-leaf clovers and poison ivy?

A: A rash of good luck.

....

Q: What do you get if you cross a vampire with a blizzard?

A: Frostbite.

....

Q: What do you get when you cross a man in a new suit with a crocodile?

A: A snappy dresser.

WHAT DO YOU CALL?

Q: What do you call a fairy who hasn't taken a bath in weeks?
A: Stinker-bell.

Q: What do you call a greasy chicken?
A: A slick chick.

Q: What do you call a rabbit with fleas?
A: Bugs Bunny.

Q: What do you call Frosty the Snowman in July?
A: A puddle.

14

Q: What do you call it when a lamb sneaks up on someone?

A: A lam-bush.

Q: What do you call a boy named Lee whom nobody ever talks to?

A: Lone-lee.

WHY?

Q: Why do bees have sticky hair?

A: Because they use a honeycomb.

Q: Why do hummingbirds hum?

A: Because they don't know the words.

Q: Why did King Kong climb the Empire State Building?

A: Because he was too big to take the elevator.

Q: Why can't bikes stand up by themselves?
A: Because they're two tired.

Q: Why is it a good idea to plant bulbs in your garden?
A: So the worms can see where they are going.

Q: Why do lions eat raw meat?
A: Because they never learned how to cook.

Q: Why isn't a bank a good place to keep a secret?
A: Because it's filled with tellers.

Q: Why do mummies tell no secrets?
A: Because they like to keep things under wraps.

Q: Why shouldn't you tell a secret to a pig?
A: Because it's a squealer.

Q: Why did the girls wear bathing suits to school?
A: They rode in a car-pool.

Q: Why do dragons sleep all day?
A: Because they like to hunt knights.

Q: Why couldn't the sailors play cards?
A: Because the captain was standing on the deck.

Q: Why is an island like the letter T?
A: Because it lies in the middle of water.

Q: Why is it hard for a ladybug to hide?
A: Because she's always spotted.

Q: Why does a ballerina wear a tutu?

A: Because a one-one's too small and a three-three's too big.

Q: Why would a heart be a good musical instrument?

A: It has a great beat.

Q: Why do geese fly south for the winter?

A: Because it's too far to walk.

Q: Why was Snow White chosen to be a judge?

A: Because everyone said she was the fairest one of all.

Q: Why was the picture sent to jail?

A: It was framed.

Q: Why did the robber take a bath before he stole from the bank?

A: He wanted to make a clean getaway.

Q: Why did the chicken cross the road?

A: To get to the other side.

....

Q: Why did the frog cross the road?

A: To see what the chicken was doing.

....

Q: Why didn't the skeleton cross the road?

A: It didn't have the guts.

Q: Why did the man run around his bed?

A: To catch up on his sleep.

WHO?

Q: Who never gets his hair wet in the shower?
A: A bald man.

Q: Who can shave all day but still grow a beard?
A: A barber.

Q: Who is a father's child and a mother's child, but no one's son?
A: A daughter.

HOW MANY?

Q: How many months have 28 days?
A: All of them.

Q: How many letters are in the alphabet?
A: Eleven.

Q: How many feet are in a yard?
A: That depends on how many people are standing in it.

WHERE?

Q: Where does a sheep get a haircut?
A: At the baa-baa shop.

Q: Where can everyone find money when they look for it?
A: In the dictionary.

Q: Where is the best place to hide a chocolate?
A: In your mouth.

Q: Where do you find forests without trees, roads without cars, and cities without people?
A: On a map.

Q: If six people were under one umbrella, why didn't any of them get wet?
A: Because it wasn't raining.

Q: If you drop a yellow hat in the Red Sea, what does it become?
A: Wet.

Q: If two is company and three's a crowd, what is four and five?
A: Nine.

Q: If dogs have fleas, what do sheep have?
A: Fleece.

Q: When is a car not a car?
A: When it turns into a parking lot.

Q: When is a door not a door?
A: When it's ajar.

Q: When is the ocean friendliest?
A: When it waves.

Q: When is a green book not a green book?
A: When it's read.